Mushroom Recipes

A Wonderful Cookbook of
Mushroom Dishes

Table of Contents

Introduction

There are so many types of mushrooms available, but what are the best ways to select and cook them?

While mushrooms can look a lot different from each other, many are the same varieties, at different life stages. They may also be planted with a different strain, which also affects their appearance and flavor.

Young mushrooms of the most common variety are often called button mushrooms. Their browner, more mature relatives may be baby Bella or Cremini mushrooms. Portobello's are not picked till they have reached their full maturity, which is why they're larger.

When you select mushrooms to use in cooking or salads, choose those with unblemished, firm caps. They should look plump and their stem should still be attached. If they have even a hint of sliminess, don't choose them.

Mushrooms are especially tasty when you sauté them. It's easy to do. Just heat a couple tbsp. of oil on med. heat. Add the mushrooms and cook for 8-10 minutes. Be sure to stir them.

You can grill Portobello mushrooms, since they are larger and have a meaty texture. It only takes 4-6 minutes to grill them well. Try new types of mushrooms and cook them to their best taste!

Mushrooms lend a wonderful taste to breakfast. Here are some recipes...

1 – Artichoke and Mushroom Breakfast Bake

This breakfast recipe works especially well since the prep work doesn't take long. It makes an attractive vegetarian dish, or you could add small smoked sausages if you have meat lovers at your breakfast table.

Makes 12 Servings

Cooking + Prep Time: 1 hour 20 minutes

Ingredients:

- 3 cups of frozen and thawed hash browns, shredded
- 2 tbsp. of melted butter, unsalted
- 1/2 tsp. of salt, kosher
- 2 1/2 cups of sliced mushrooms, fresh
- 1 x 14-oz. can of rinsed, drained, quartered artichoke hearts, packed in water
- 3 cups of cheddar cheese shreds
- 12 eggs, large
- 1 3/4 cups of milk, 2%
- 1 x 4-oz. can of drained green chilies, chopped

Instructions:

1. Preheat the oven to 350F. Place the potatoes in lightly greased 13 x 9-inch casserole dish. Drizzle using 1 tbsp. of butter. Sprinkle with a bit of salt. Bake for 20 to 25 minutes, till browned lightly.

2. Sauté mushrooms in the rest of your butter in small sized skillet till they are tender. Then place the artichokes on some paper towels and pat them dry.

3. Sprinkle the cheese, mushrooms and artichokes over potatoes. Whisk chilies, eggs and milk in large sized bowl. Pour this mixture over the cheese.

4. Leave casserole uncovered and bake for 40 to 45 minutes. Knife inserted in middle should come back clean. Allow the dish to set for five minutes. Serve.

2 – Mushroom and Potato Breakfast

My whole family loves this breakfast dish, since the flavors of bacon and mushroom accent each other so well. It's a really easy recipe, too.

Makes 6 Servings

Cooking + Prep Time: 45 minutes

Ingredients:

- 5 potatoes, medium
- 1 lb. of diced mushrooms, fresh
- 1/2 onion, large, cubed
- To cook: oil, olive
- Salt, kosher, as desired
- 1/2 cup of bacon crisps

Instructions:

1. Cube the onions and sauté them in oiled skillet till they have softened and started turning golden-brown.

2. Add diced mushrooms to onions. Maintain med-high heat. Sauté till mushrooms begin to turn golden.

3. Add cubed potatoes to skillet. Season lightly with kosher salt. Stir ingredients now and then so you have created a golden crust. It should be done on all four sides.

4. After potatoes have cooked completely through, add bacon crisps. Stir and combine well. Serve hot. It tastes great reheated, too, if you have leftovers.

3 – Sausage and Mushroom Breakfast Quiche

This breakfast is savory, warm and it pleases everyone. That includes whomever cooks it, since it comes together so easily, which is helpful on those busy mornings we all have.

Makes 2 full quiches with 6 to 8 pieces each

Cooking + Prep Time: 55 minutes

Ingredients:

- 1 lb. of bulk pork sausage, mild
- 1/4 lb. of bulk pork sausage, spicy
- 12 eggs, large
- 2 cups of cottage cheese, 4%
- 3 cups of shredded cheese, Monterey Jack
- 1 cup of mozzarella cheese shreds, part-skim
- 1/2 cup of flour, all-purpose
- 1/2 cup of melted butter, unsalted
- 1 tsp. of baking powder
- 3/4 cup of onion, chopped finely
- 2 cups of sliced mushrooms, fresh
- 1 x 4-oz. can of drained green chilies, chopped
- Optional: Parmesan cheese, grated
- Sweet pepper strips, red or green (or both)

Instructions:

1. In large sized skillet on med. heat, cook the sausage till it is not pink any more. Drain it well.

2. Beat cheeses, eggs, butter, baking powder and flour in large sized bowl. Add and stir sausage, chilies, onions and mushrooms.

3. Transfer mixture to 2 x 9" lightly greased baking dishes. The mixture should fill them both up. Sprinkle them with some Parmesan cheese, as desired.

4. Bake in 375F oven for 30-35 minutes. Knife inserted in middle should come back clan. Garnish as desired and serve.

4 – Mushroom Onion Scrambled Eggs

The cheese and onion give these scrambled eggs a creaminess you won't find in many dishes. You can serve it for breakfast or brunch. We use a variety of mushroom types, and this dish can be served with toast, too.

Makes 2 Servings

Cooking + Prep Time: 40 minutes

Ingredients:

- 1 1/2 tbsp. of oil, olive
- 1 x 8-oz. pkg. of sliced mushrooms, fresh

- 1 sliced onion, medium
- 1 minced garlic clove
- 1 1/2 tbsp. of seasoning, Italian
- 5 eggs, large
- 2 tbsp. of herb garlic cheese spread
- Salt, kosher, as desired
- Pepper, ground, as desired
- 1/3 cup of mozzarella cheese shreds

Instructions:

1. Heat the oil in skillet on med. heat. Stir while cooking the garlic, mushrooms and onions till onions brown. This usually takes 12-15 minutes. Add Italian seasoning.

2. Beat the eggs with the cheese spread in med. bowl. Expect the mixture to end up a bit chunky. Season as desired.

3. Pour the eggs in the skillet on top of the mushroom mixture. Stir while cooking till eggs have almost set – this usually only takes a minute or so.

4. Fold the mozzarella into the eggs until it barely melts, about 25-35 seconds. Serve hot.

5 – Baked Mushroom Omelet

This is another mushroom dish that was intended to be used for breakfast, but it can fill in at lunch or supper, too. The egg picks up wonderful flavors from the bacon, cheese and mushrooms.

Makes 4 Servings

Cooking + Prep Time: 1/2 hour

Ingredients:

- 1/2 lb. of sliced mushrooms, fresh
- 2 tbsp. of butter, unsalted

- 2 tbsp. of flour, all-purpose
- 6 eggs, large
- 1/3 cup of milk, whole
- 1/8 tsp. of pepper, black, ground
- 1 1/2 cups of cheddar cheese shreds
- 1/2 cup of bacon bits, real

Instructions:

1. Sauté the mushrooms in unsalted butter in small sized skillet till they have become tender, then drain them.

2. Combine milk, eggs, pepper and flour in medium bowl till the mixture is smooth. Add and stir 1 cup of cheese, plus mushrooms and bacon. Pour this into lightly greased 8" square casserole dish. Sprinkle with the rest of the cheese.

3. Leave casserole uncovered and bake in 375F oven for 15-20 minutes, till eggs have set completely. Serve hot.

Here are some great mushroom recipes for lunch, dinner, appetizers or side dishes...

6 – Parmesan and Garlic Mushrooms

The mushrooms in this wonderful dish are sautéed in buttery garlic till they're tender. Then you'll toss them in this AMAZING parmesan cheese sauce. You can serve alone, as a side dish or on the top of meat.

Makes 5 Servings

Cooking + Prep Time: 15 minutes

Ingredients:

- 2 tbsp. of butter, unsalted
- 1 tbsp. of oil, olive
- 8 oz. of mushrooms, white - sliced or whole, as desired
- 2 minced garlic cloves
- 1/2 cup of cream, heavy
- 1/4 cup of parmesan cheese, grated
- 2 oz. of softened cream cheese
- 1 tsp. of seasoning blend, Italian
- 1/2 tsp. of salt, kosher
- 1/4 tsp. of pepper, ground

Instructions:

1. Add oil and butter to medium skillet on med-high heat. Add garlic and mushrooms. Sauté till they are tender.

2. Add cream, cream cheese, parmesan cheese, kosher salt, ground pepper and Italian seasoning to garlic and mushrooms. Stir in and heat till sauce is smooth and bubbly. Serve promptly.

7 – Sautéed Mushrooms

Be sure to buy plenty of mushrooms for this dish, because they tend to get eaten as soon as they are prepared. If you like, you can use oregano instead of thyme, and deglaze your pan with wine after the mushrooms cook.

Makes 4 Servings

Cooking + Prep Time: 40 minutes

Ingredients:

- 2 tbsp. of butter, unsalted
- 1/2 tbsp. of oil, olive
- 1/2 tbsp. of vinegar, balsamic
- 1 minced garlic clove
- 1/8 tsp. of oregano, dried
- 1 lb. of sliced button mushrooms

Instructions:

1. Melt the butter in oil in large sized skillet on med. heat. Add and stir vinegar, mushrooms, garlic and oregano. Sauté for 15-25 minutes, till very tender. Serve.

8 – Red Rice and Mushroom Stuffing with Carrots

This rice and mushroom stuffing recipe will be welcomed at your next Thanksgiving dinner! It has fewer carbs than traditional stuffing. You don't have to wait till the holidays to serve it, though.

Makes 8 Servings

Cooking + Prep Time: 55 minutes

Ingredients:

- 2 pounds of peeled carrots, lengthways halved cut in 1 1/2" pieces
- 5 tbsp. of oil, olive
- 1 tbsp. of chopped rosemary, fresh
- 3 cups of stock, vegetable
- 1 1/2 cups of rice, red
- 3 bay leaves
- 2 tbsp. of chopped thyme, fresh
- 1 chopped onion, large
- 1 1/2 pounds of sliced mushrooms, mixed types
- 3 chopped garlic cloves
- 1/3 cup of chopped parsley, flat-leaf, fresh

Instructions:

1. Preheat oven to 425F. Toss carrots and rosemary with 2 tbsp. of oil on cookie sheet. Season as desired. Spread in one even, single layer. Roast till they are tender. This usually takes 25 minutes to 1/2 hour.

2. In med. sauce pan with lid, bring stock to boil. Add bay leaves and rice. Add salt as desired. Bring back to boil. Reduce the heat to med-low. Cover. Simmer till rice

becomes tender. This generally takes 25-30 minutes. Use a fork to fluff the rice and discard bay leaves.

3. Heat 1 tbsp. of oil on med. heat in skillet. Add onion and season as desired. Stir often while cooking until it is soft. Transfer onions to bowl. Add thyme and mix. In same skillet, heat the rest of your oil on med-high. Add mushrooms and season as desired. Stir often while cooking till they start browning. Add garlic and stir till mushrooms have browned.

4. Mix parsley, mushroom mixture, rice and carrots in large sized bowl. Serve.

9 – Slow Cooker Roast Beef and Mushrooms

The beef in this recipe falls off the bone – it's that tender – and the mushrooms accent the meat so well. You can even shred leftovers (if there are any) and use them for sandwiches.

Makes 8 Servings

Cooking + Prep Time: 15 minutes + 9-10 hours slow cooker time

Ingredients:

- 1 lb. of sliced mushrooms, fresh
- 1 x 4-lb. roast, standing beef rib
- 1 x 1 1/4-oz. pkg. of soup mix, onion
- 1 x 12-fluid oz. bottle of beer
- Black pepper, ground

Instructions:

1. Place mushrooms in bottom of your slow cooker. Set roast on top of them. Sprinkle soup mix over roast. Pour beer over all ingredients in slow cooker. Season with ground pepper.

2. Set the slow cooker to the LOW setting. Cook for nine to 10 hours, till meat is tender. Serve.

10 – Steaks with Red Wine and Mushroom Gravy

These steaks are classic additions to comfort food menus. This version uses grated onions and dry bread crumbs and a simple mushroom gravy that is perfect with the steaks.

Makes 4 Servings

Cooking + Prep Time: 40 minutes

Ingredients:

- 1 1/4 lbs. of ground beef, extra lean
- 1/4 tsp. of pepper, ground

- 1/2 tsp. of salt, kosher
- 1/4 tsp. of salt, seasoned
- 3 tbsp. of bread crumbs, dry, fine
- 2 tbsp. of milk, 2%
- 1 slightly beaten egg, large
- 2 tbsp. of onion, grated
- 2 tbsp. of oil, vegetable
- 1/2 to 3/4 cup of mushrooms, sliced thinly
- 2 tbsp. of flour, all-purpose
- 1 cup of broth, beef
- Optional: 1 tbsp. of red wine, dry

Instructions:

1. Combine the beef, bread crumbs, seasoned salt, kosher salt and ground pepper. Shape the meat into four oval-shaped patties.

2. Heat the oil in skillet on med. heat. Fry patties for five to seven minutes per side, till they have cooked completely through. Remove the patties to a warm plate. Keep them warm.

3. Pour off drippings except for 2 tbsp. Add mushroom and onions to drippings left in skillet. Cook till they are tender.

4. Add flour to mushroom-onion drippings in skillet. Cook for a minute or two more.

5. Add broth, milk and (if you're using it) wine. Stir while cooking till gravy thickens.

6. Pour gravy over streaks. Serve with a veggie side.

11 – Lemon Chicken with Mushrooms

This simple, quick lemon chicken and mushroom recipe only requires a few ingredients, and some may be in your pantry already. It's super delicious for such a simple dish.

Makes 2 Servings

Cooking + Prep Time: 25 minutes

Ingredients:

- 2 chicken breasts, skinless, boneless
- 1/2 cup of fresh lemon juice

- 1 tbsp. of oil, olive
- 1 tsp. of pepper, lemon
- 2 tbsp. of mushrooms, your choice of type
- 1/2 tsp. of basil, dried
- 1/2 tsp. of oregano, dried
- 1/10 tsp. of salt, kosher

Instructions:

1. Place the chicken in large zipper lock plastic bag. Add oil, lemon juice, salt, oregano, basil and lemon pepper. Shake bag and make sure mixture covers all the chicken. Allow to marinate in your refrigerator for at least 1/2 hour or as long as eight hours.

2. Heat large skillet on med-high.

3. Remove chicken from marinade bag. Place in heated skillet. Discard extra marinade.

4. Cook the chicken for six or seven minutes each side, and flip when half-way done. Continue to cook till chicken has reached 165F on internal thermometer. Serve it hot.

12 – Barley and Mushroom Casserole

This casserole with mushrooms **Makes** a tasty side dish that goes especially well with roast beef or grilled steaks. The mushrooms provide the barley with an earthy flavor that is very appealing.

Makes 6 Servings

Cooking + Prep Time: 2 hours 10 minutes

Ingredients:

- 1/4 cup of butter, unsalted
- 8 oz. of fresh mushrooms, sliced
- 1 cup of onion, chopped
- 1 minced garlic clove
- 1 cup of barley, medium
- 1/2 tsp. +/- of salt, kosher, as desired
- 1/8 tsp. of pepper, ground
- 4 cups of stock, chicken, low sodium

Instructions:

1. Heat oven to 350 degrees F. Butter a 3-quart baking dish.

2. Melt the butter in large sized skillet on med-low. Add the onion and mushrooms. Sauté till browned lightly.

3. Add garlic. Cook for a minute more.

4. Add barley. Stir while cooking till browned slightly.

5. Add kosher salt and ground pepper. Turn into baking dish.

6. Pour broth into skillet. Heat till it is hot.

7. Pour broth over barley mixture. Combine thoroughly.

8. Cover baking dish. Bake at 350F for 1 1/2 hours, till barley becomes tender. Add additional water or broth if you need to. Serve hot.

13 – Mushroom Manicotti Casserole

Some of my family refers to this dish as an Italian casserole. Whatever you call it, the meal is easy to prepare and a favorite with everyone.

Makes 8 Servings

Cooking + Prep Time: 45 minutes

Ingredients:

- 1 lb. of pasta – rigatoni
- 1 lb. of beef, ground
- 1 lb. of sausage, Italian
- 1 x 8-oz. can of drained mushrooms
- 2 x 32-oz. jars of spaghetti sauce
- 1 1/2 lbs. of mozzarella cheese shreds
- Pepperoni, sliced thinly

Instructions:

1. Preheat the oven to 350F.

2. Bring large sized pot of salted water up to a boil. Add rigatoni. Cook till it is al dente. Drain pasta and set it aside.

3. Brown the Italian sausage and ground beef in large sized skillet on med. heat. Remove the meats to baking dish. Stir cooked pasta, mushrooms and spaghetti sauce into baking dish. Sprinkle pepperoni and cheese on top of mixture.

4. Bake at 350F till cheese is bubbly and brown, about 20-25 minutes. Serve.

14 – Indian Mushroom Curry

This dish originated in Northern India. The gravy color is red, but that doesn't mean it's an especially spicy or hot dish. The curry incorporates garlic and ginger for a delectable taste.

Makes 2 Servings

Cooking + Prep Time: 45 minutes

Ingredients:

- 1 quartered onion, large
- 3 quartered tomatoes, medium
- 2 chilies, green +/- as desired
- 5 garlic cloves
- 1" piece of fresh ginger
- 2 tsp. of coriander powder
- 3 tbsp. of oil, sunflower
- 1 tsp. of cumin powder
- 2 cups of mushrooms, button, cleaned and halved
- 1/2 tsp. of red chili powder (optional)
- 1/4 tsp. of turmeric powder
- 1 tsp. of garam masala Asian spice blend
- A dash of salt, +/- as desired
- 4 tbsp. of unsweetened yogurt, thick
- For garnishing: 1/4 cup of coriander, fresh

Instructions:

1. Wash vegetables well, removing dirt and any pesticides that may linger on them.

2. Place quartered tomatoes and onions, then chilies, garlic and ginger in food processor. Grind into smooth paste.

3. Heat oil in deep pan over med. heat. Add mixture from step 2, then powdered spices. Stir while frying everything till oil starts separating from garam masala. Stir mixture quite often, preventing masala from becoming stuck or burnt.

4. When masala has finished cooking, add mushrooms. Stir them gently. Season with kosher salt as desired. Add 1/2 cup of warm, filtered water.

5. Cook mixture together till mushrooms become soft. They should NOT be over-cooked or pulpy, though. Remove food from heat. Add and stir yogurt till blended well, to give it a rich and creamy texture.

6. Garnish dish with chopped coriander. Serve with rice, if you like.

15 – Pork Chops with Mushrooms

This is a delicious recipe and it's my family's favorite pork chop recipe, ever. The veggie prep can take a little time, but other than that, the recipe is pretty easy.

Makes 4 Servings

Cooking + Prep Time: 3/4 hour

Ingredients:

- 4 pork chops
- Kosher salt ground pepper, as desired
- 1 pinch +/- garlic salt, as desired
- 1 chopped onion
- 1/2 lb. of sliced mushrooms, fresh
- 1 x 10 3/4 oz. can of cream of mushroom soup, condensed

Instructions:

1. Season the pork chops using garlic salt, kosher salt and ground pepper, as desired.

2. Brown chops in large sized skillet on med-high. Add mushrooms and onion. Sauté for a minute. Pour the soup over the chops. Cover the skillet. Reduce temperature down to med-low. Simmer for 25-30 minutes till chops have cooked through. Serve hot.

16 – Savory Mushroom Strudel

Eastern Europe is home to many aromatic, pungent wild mushrooms, and this is a dish from that region. Mushroom strudel is a wonderful vegetarian main course with a green salad on the side.

Makes 4 Servings

Cooking + Prep Time: 1 hour 5 minutes

Ingredients:

- 2 tbsp. of butter, unsalted
- 1/4 cup of oil, olive

- 1 chopped shallot, large
- 2 chopped garlic cloves
- 1 1/2 lbs. of mushrooms, fresh, assorted types
- Salt, sea
- Pepper, ground
- 2 tbsp. each of chives, parsley, tarragon and thyme
- 1 egg, large, + 1 egg yolk, large, beaten well together
- 1 sheet of puff pastry, thawed
- 1 egg, large + 1 tsp. of water for the egg wash

Instructions:

1. Heat the oil and butter in large sized skillet. Add garlic and shallots. Cook and soften. Add the sliced mushrooms.

2. Season using sea salt and ground pepper. Cook on low heat till tender. If any juices exude, turn the heat up and cook till they have evaporated.

3. Stir in 3/4 of your herbs. Remove skillet from stove top burner. Spread the mushrooms on a baking sheet so they can dry and completely cool, which takes about 1/2 hour.

4. When mushrooms have cooled and dried, transfer them to large sized bowl. Combine with the egg and egg yolk mixture.

5. Move the rack to center of the oven. Heat the oven to 400F.

6. Place the puff pastry on baking paper-lined, rimmed cookie sheet. Roll out creases, if any. Brush the surface with the egg wash. Sprinkle remaining herbs over the top.

7. Evenly spread the mushrooms over the first 3/4 of the pastry. Leave a 1" border at edges.

8. Flip edge nearest you over. Lay on top 1/4 so pastry touches pastry. It will encase the mushrooms fully in a cylinder shape. Don't try to roll it in a pinwheel for the strudel, or the interior pastry won't bake.

9. Move the strudel to middle of cookie sheet. Tuck the ends in. Brush the surface with the egg wash.

10. Use back of a knife to run a crisscross pattern over the strudel. Cut some of the pastry out, in any design you choose. Egg wash your designs.

11. Bake pastry till it is puffed and golden brown in color. This can take between 15 and 30 minutes. Allow to rest for two minutes or more, then slice and serve.

17 – Slow Cooker Mushroom Stuffing

This recipe offers a simple way to make more stuffing to serve larger groups. It saves on the stove space, since you'll cook it in your slow cooker. The result is very moist and tasty.

Makes 16 Servings

Cooking + Prep Time: 1 hour 25 minutes + 4-8 hours slow cooker time

Ingredients:

- 1 cup of margarine or butter
- 2 cups of onion, chopped
- 2 cups of celery, chopped
- 1/4 cup of chopped parsley, fresh
- 12 oz. of mushrooms, sliced
- 12 cups of bread cubes, dried
- 1 tsp. of seasoning, poultry
- 1 1/2 tsp. of sage, dried
- 1 tsp. of thyme, dried
- 1/2 tsp. of marjoram, dried
- 1 1/2 tsp. of salt, kosher
- 1/2 tsp. of pepper, black, ground
- 4 1/2 cups of broth, chicken, +/- as desired
- 2 beaten eggs, large

Instructions:

1. Melt the margarine or butter in skillet on med. heat. Cook the parsley, mushrooms, celery and onions in the butter, frequently stirring.

2. Spoon the cooked veggies over the bread cubes in large sized bowl. Season using the kosher salt, ground pepper,

marjoram, thyme, sage and poultry seasoning. Add some broth for moistening the bread cubes. Mix the eggs in, as well. Transfer the mixture to your slow cooker. Cover.

3. Cook on the HIGH setting for 45-50 minutes. Reduce setting to LOW. Cook for four to eight hours. Serve hot.

18 – Creamy Mushroom Vegan Pasta

There aren't a lot of vegan dishes that are also creamy, but it happens in this recipe. Pasta dishes are quite popular, and this one has a mushroom sauce, rather than one that is tomato-based.

Makes 4 Servings

Cooking + Prep Time: 25 minutes

Ingredients:

- 1 lb. of pasta, long-noodle, like linguini or angel hair
- 1/4 cup of soy margarine, dairy-free
- 2 minced garlic cloves, large
- 16 oz. of halved mushrooms, Cremini
- 1 tbsp. of flour, all-purpose
- 1 cup of soy milk, plain
- 1/4 cup of sour cream, dairy-free
- 1/4 tsp. of salt, kosher, + extra as desired
- Pepper, black, ground, as desired

Instructions:

1. Bring large sized pot of lightly salted water to rolling boil. Add the pasta. Cook till al dente. Drain pasta. Set it aside.

2. In large sized pan, heat 2 tbsp. soy margarine on med-high. Add mushrooms and garlic. Cook till mushrooms are soft and fragrant, or about three to four minutes. Don't overcook. Transfer mushrooms and garlic to large sized bowl. Set it aside.

3. In same large pan on med-high, heat last 2 tbsp. of soy margarine and flour. Whisk constantly so they combine, for about 40 seconds to a minute. Don't allow them to burn.

4. Continue stirring constantly, and gradually add soy milk till you have a smooth mixture. Add sour cream, kosher salt and ground pepper. Stir well till combined. Add garlic and mushrooms to sauce. Cook for a couple more minutes.

5. Remove pan from the heat. Add pasta to sauce. Toss and coat noodles. Place pasta on individual plates. Add ground pepper as desired. Serve promptly.

19 – Stuffed Mushrooms

These delectable mushrooms taste like those you might serve at a restaurant. They're a favorite in my home and may be in yours, too.

Makes 12 Servings

Cooking + Prep Time: 50 minutes

Ingredients:

- 12 whole mushrooms, fresh
- 1 tbsp. of oil, vegetable
- 1 tbsp. of garlic, minced
- 1 x 8-oz. pkg. of softened cream cheese
- 1/4 cup of parmesan cheese, grated
- 1/4 tsp. of pepper, ground
- 1/4 tsp. of cayenne pepper, ground
- 1/4 tsp. of onion powder

Instructions:

1. Preheat the oven to 350F. Spray cookie sheet with non-stick spray.

2. Clean mushrooms. Break off the stems carefully. Chop the stems finely and discard the tough ends of the stems.

3. Heat the oil in large sized skillet on med. heat. Next, add chopped stems of mushrooms and the garlic to skillet. Fry till all moisture is gone. Don't allow the garlic to burn. Set the mixture aside for cooling.

4. When the mushroom and garlic mixture isn't hot anymore, stir in the parmesan cheese, cream cheese, cayenne pepper,

ground pepper and onion powder. This new mixture should appear very thick.

5. Fill the mushroom caps with this stuffing, generously. Arrange caps on the cookie sheet you prepared above.

6. Bake the filled mushroom caps at 350F for 20 minutes, or till mushrooms are very hot and liquid begins forming under the caps. Remove from oven. Serve hot.

20 – Cream of Mushroom Dairy-Free Soup

This soup recipe is so tasty that no one believes how simple it is to make. I can't tell you how many times I've been asked for the recipe. It's especially good when paired with crusty bread.

Makes 8 Servings

Cooking + Prep Time: 1 hour

Ingredients:

- 3 tbsp. of oil, olive
- 1/4 cup of chopped garlic, fresh
- 2 chopped Vidalia onions, large
- 4 chopped celery stalks
- 2 1/2 lbs. of chopped mushrooms, Cremini
- 2 tbsp. of chopped parsley, fresh
- 2 tsp. of dried thyme
- 1/2 cup of sherry
- 7 cups of vegetable broth
- 1 cup of sour cream, dairy-free
- 1 1/2 cup of soy milk, plain + extra as needed
- 1 pinch of salt, kosher, as desired
- 1 pinch of pepper, black, as desired

Instructions:

1. Heat oil in large sized sauce pan on med-high. Once oil is hot, add celery, garlic and onions. Stir often till onions are fragrant and soft, or about five minutes.

2. Add mushrooms, sherry, thyme and parsley. Stir often while cooking, till mushrooms have softened. Add veggie

broth and bring mixture to boil. Reduce heat and allow to simmer for about 10 minutes.

3. Transfer soup carefully to large stock pot. Use food processor and work in batches to process the soup till it is smooth. Portion soy milk and soy cream into food processor as you mix, till you have used it all, and the soup is pureed.

4. Transfer soup back to sauce pan. Heat to desired temperature and consistency. Season as desired. Serve hot.

21 – Mushroom Scaloppini

This dish is stunning in the way it is presented, and it has a lively rich taste, too. The ingredient blend is so creative. It's an excellent side dish.

Makes 8 Servings

Cooking + Prep Time: 35 minutes

Ingredients:

- 1 lb. of pasta, angel hair

- 1/4 cup of oil, olive
- 2 minced garlic cloves
- 2 minced shallot bulbs
- 1 lb. of sliced mushrooms, shiitake
- 1/2 tsp. of thyme, dried
- 1/2 cup of wine, white
- 4 x 6-oz. cans of drained, chopped artichoke hearts, pre-marinated
- 1/4 cup of capers, small

Instructions:

1. Bring large sized pot of salted, filtered water to boil. Add the pasta. Cook till it is al dente and drain.

2. Heat the oil in heavy, large skillet on low heat. Sweat the shallots and garlic till they have started to become more aromatic.

3. Raise heat up to med. Add thyme and mushrooms. Sauté till the mushrooms have begun softening. Deglaze the pan with white wine. Simmer for two minutes. Add and stir capers and artichokes. Simmer for a few more minutes. Pour this mushroom mixture on pasta. Serve.

22 – Mushroom-Sauced Fish Fillets

This recipe is perfect for a quick and easy family meal. Its combination of thyme, mushrooms, onions and sour cream with lemon juice is a great sauce for the flaky, tender fish.

Makes 4 Servings

Cooking + Prep Time: 3/4 hour

Ingredients:

- 2 tbsp. of butter, unsalted
- 1 1/2 cups of Cremini mushrooms, sliced
- 1 chopped onion
- 3 minced garlic cloves
- 2 tbsp. of flour, all-purpose
- 1 tsp. of thyme leaves, dried
- 1/2 tsp. of salt, kosher
- 1/8 tsp. of pepper, WHITE
- 1 cup of milk, 2%
- 1/2 cup of sour cream
- 2 tbsp. of lemon juice, fresh
- 1 tsp. of lemon peel, grated
- 1 1/2 lbs. of fish fillets

Instructions:

1. Preheat oven to 350F. Grease medium glass casserole dish. Set dish aside.

2. Melt butter in medium sized sauce pan on med. heat. When it begins sizzling a little, add garlic, mushrooms and onion. Cook the veggies, frequently stirring, till they become tender and liquid has evaporated.

3. Add thyme, flour, kosher salt WHITE pepper to sauce pan. Stir and cook for a couple more minutes. Add sour cream and milk. Stir and cook till sauce thickens and bubbles.

4. Remove pan from heat. Add lemon peel and juice. Place fish in casserole dish. Cover with the sauce. Bake for 15 to 20 minutes, till fish has been cooked to 145F or higher. It should also flake easily when you test it with a fork. Serve.

23 – Chicken with Leek and Mushroom Sauce

White wine and leeks add a wonderful gourmet touch to a dish that's quick enough to make on a work night. It's especially tasty served over quinoa.

Makes 8 Servings

Cooking + Prep Time: 45 minutes

Ingredients:

- 1 tbsp. of oil, olive
- 8 chicken thighs, skinless, boneless
- 4 cups of sliced mushrooms, baby Bella
- 2 sliced leeks
- 2/3 cup of white wine, dry
- 1 1/2 cups of chicken broth, reduced sodium
- 2 tsp. of corn starch
- 2/3 cup of sour cream, low fat
- 1 1/2 tsp. of mustard, Dijon
- Salt, kosher pepper, ground, as desired

Instructions:

1. Heat the oil in large sized skillet on med-high. Add the chicken. Cook it till it has browned well and isn't pink in middle anymore. Transfer the chicken to plate. Cover it and keep the chicken warm.

2. Add the leeks and mushrooms to skillet. Stir often while cooking on med. heat till most moisture has evaporated. Mushrooms should have begun browning, as well.

3. Add the wine. Cook for a minute or so. Mix the corn starch and broth together in medium bowl. Add to skillet. Cook till mixture thickens. Add and stir mustard and sour cream. Stir while cooking till combined well. Season as desired.

4. Nestle the chicken into sauce. Cook till internal thermometer reads 165F or higher. Serve.

24 – Mushroom and Vegetable Burger

The term "veggie burger" isn't elegant enough for this dish, since it **Makes** it sound so ordinary. It's not! Instead of being boring or bland, this mushroom veggie burger is hefty and spicy.

Makes 4 Servings

Cooking + Prep Time: 45 minutes

Ingredients:

- 3 tbsp. of oil, olive
- 1 1/2 lbs. of chopped mushrooms
- 1/2 cup of chopped onion
- 6 minced garlic cloves
- 2/3 cup of oats, rolled
- 1/3 cup of parmesan cheese shreds
- 3/4 cup of bread crumbs
- 2 beaten eggs, large
- 1 tbsp. of parsley, fresh
- 1 tsp. of oregano, dried
- 1/2 tsp. of salt, kosher

Instructions:

1. Heat just 1 tbsp. of oil in large sized sauce pan. Sauté garlic, mushrooms and onions on med. heat for 8-10 minutes, till liquid has boiled off and mushrooms have begun sautéing.

2. Add mushroom mixture to large bowl with oregano, parsley, eggs, bread crumbs, parmesan cheese, kosher salt and ground pepper. Combine thoroughly. Allow bowl to sit

for 12-15 minutes, so flavors can develop. Shape mixture into patties.

3. Heat the other 2 tbsp. of oil in large skillet on med. heat. Fry patties. Cook five minutes or so per side, till they are a golden brown in color. Serve with burger toppings.

25 – Mushroom Asparagus Frittata

This is a wonderful lunch dish, and extra tasty with its combination of mushrooms and asparagus. You'll start it on the stove top and finish it in the oven. It has great taste when reheated, too.

Makes 4 Servings

Cooking + Prep Time: 45 minutes

Ingredients:

- 2 tbsp. of oil, olive
- 1 peeled garlic clove
- 1/2 trimmed, 1"-cut bunch of asparagus
- 1 x 9-oz. pkg. of sliced mushrooms, fresh
- Salt, kosher, as desired
- Black pepper, ground, as desired
- 1/3 cup of white wine, dry
- 4 large eggs, free-range
- 1/3 cup of milk, 2%
- 3 tbsp. of parmesan cheese, grated
- 1 tbsp. of chopped parsley, fresh

Instructions:

1. Preheat oven to 350F.

2. Heat the oil in oven-safe skillet on med. heat. Cook the garlic till it starts sizzling. Add mushrooms and asparagus. Cook till they soften. Season as desired. Add white wine and discard the garlic.

3. Mix the milk, eggs, 2 tbsp. of parmesan cheese, kosher salt, ground pepper and parsley in bowl. Pour mixture into

skillet on top of mushrooms and asparagus. Gently stir. Cook for several minutes, till eggs begin setting. Sprinkle with last 1 tbsp. of the parmesan cheese. Transfer skillet with mixture into oven.

4. Bake at 350F till frittata is risen and has set. This usually takes 18-20 minutes. Allow to cool a bit. Serve.

26 – Cream of Mushroom Vegan Soup

This soup flavor is often used for a base for home-made recipes. It works well in that role, but it's also very tasty all alone. Since this is a vegan recipe, it should appeal to the non-meat-eaters of your family.

Makes 4 Servings

Cooking + Prep Time: 1 hour 20 minutes

Ingredients:

- 3/4 lb. of sliced mushrooms, fresh
- 1/2 diced small yellow or white onion
- 2 minced garlic cloves
- 1 tbsp. of margarine, vegan
- 3 cups of broth, vegetable
- 2 tbsp. of flour, all-purpose
- 1 cup of sour cream substitute, non-dairy
- 1 cup of milk, soy

Instructions:

1. Sauté garlic, mushrooms and onion in large pot in the vegan margarine for several minutes, till onions become soft.

2. Lower heat to med-low. Add broth. Cover pot. Allow to simmer for 45 minutes or longer.

3. Add flour, soy milk and sour cream. Combine well.

4. Let mixture simmer for 20-30 more minutes, till soup thickens. Season as desired and serve.

27 – Tilapia and Oyster Mushrooms

In this recipe, you'll pan fry the tilapia fillets and serve them with an easy cream sauce including oyster mushrooms. Yes, the sauce is simple – but it's still delicious.

Makes 4 Servings

Cooking + Prep Time: 1/2 hour

Ingredients:

- 2 tbsp. of butter, unsalted
- 3 cups of de-stemmed, sliced oyster mushrooms, fresh

- 1 cup of whipping cream, heavy
- Kosher salt ground pepper, as desired
- 4 x 8-oz. tilapia fillets
- 2 tbsp. of flour, all-purpose
- 2 tbsp. of oil, vegetable

Instructions:

1. Melt the butter in skillet on med. heat. Cook the mushrooms till they brown. Add the cream, then season as desired. Simmer till the sauce has thickened.

2. Cut the tilapia into large-sized pieces. Season as desired and dredge them in the flour.

3. Heat the oil in skillet on med. heat. Cook the tilapia till browned and cooked through. Arrange on plate. Cover with creamy mushroom sauce. Serve.

28 – Mushroom Risotto

This is a delectable variation on your basic risotto. The magic itself comes from the use of mushroom stock. You can substitute veggie stock if you prefer.

Makes 6-8 Servings

Cooking + Prep Time: 45 minutes

Ingredients:

- 1 quart of stock, mushroom, chicken or vegetable
- 4 tbsp. of butter, unsalted
- 1 cup of sliced mushrooms

- 1 tbsp. of oil, vegetable
- 1 chopped shallot, medium
- 1 1/2 cups of rice, arborio
- 1/2 cup of wine, white
- 1/4 cup of grated cheese, parmesan
- 1 tbsp. of chopped parsley, Italian
- Salt, kosher, as desired

Instructions:

1. Heat stock to simmer in medium sized sauce pan. Lower heat and just keep stock hot.

2. Melt 1 tbsp. butter in sauté pan. Sauté mushrooms till soft. Remove them from stove top burner. Set them aside.

3. In heavy-bottom, large sized sauce pot, heat oil and 1 tbsp. of butter on med. heat. When butter is melted, then add shallot. Sauté for a few minutes, till it is a bit translucent.

4. Add rice to pot. Stir briskly so grains will all be coated with melted butter and oil. Sauté for about one minute longer, till you smell an aroma that is a bit nutty. Don't allow rice to brown.

5. Add wine. Stir while cooking till liquid has been absorbed fully.

6. Add ladle of hot stock to rice. Stir till it has been absorbed fully. When rice is nearly dry, add next ladle of the stock. Repeat this process till stock is all added. Add cooked mushrooms before last ladle of stock. Be sure to constantly stir so it won't scorch. As rice cooks while you're ladling stock, it will develop a creamy consistency.

7. If you don't have more stock left but rice is not yet done, add hot water as needed.

8. Add and stir last 2 tbsp. of butter, then cheese and parsley. Season as desired and serve.

29 – Sirloin and Mushrooms

In this dish, sirloin steak is served along with an easy but sophisticated sauce made with butter, shallots, white wine, tarragon and shiitake mushrooms. It's impressive but not difficult.

Makes 2 Servings

Cooking + Prep Time: 35 minutes

Ingredients:

- 1 x 12-oz. steak, sirloin
- Kosher salt, as desired

- Ground pepper, as desired
- 2 tbsp. of oil, olive, +/- as you need it
- 1/3 cup of de-stemmed, sliced cap mushrooms, shiitake
- 1/2 sliced shallot
- 1 peeled garlic clove
- 1/3 cup of white wine, dry
- 1/3 cup of broth, beef
- 1/4 cup of cubed butter
- 2 tbsp. of chopped tarragon, fresh

Instructions:

1. Season the steak on both sides as desired.

2. Heat heavy skillet on high heat. Add oil. Add steak. Cook till it starts firming up. It should be hot and a bit pink in the middle. Internal thermometer should say 140F or higher.

3. Remove steak from the skillet. Set it aside and tent with foil so it stays warm. Discard the oil still in your skillet.

4. Reduce the heat to med-low. Cook garlic, mushrooms and shallot. Stir frequently till they are softened. Pour in the

white wine. Cook till reduced slightly. Add beef broth. Reduce the heat down to low.

5. Add and stir butter, one cube after another, and stir well after each cube is added. Add and stir tarragon. Season as desired. Serve steak with mushroom sauce on top.

30 – Mushroom Pizza

Mushrooms shine in this recipe, with fontina cheese, roasted garlic and fresh mint. The result is unique, as well as delicious.

Makes 2-4 Servings

Cooking + Prep Time: 3 hours 10 minutes

Ingredients:

- 1 lb. of pizza dough, store bought
- 8 garlic cloves
- 1/4 cup of oil, olive
- Pepper, black, ground, as desired
- 1/2 lb. of mushrooms
- 1 tsp. of salt, kosher
- 1 cup of fontina cheese, grated
- 6 fresh mint leaves, optional
- 1/3 cup of grated parmesan cheese

Instructions:

1. Arrange cooking rack on lowest oven rungs. Preheat oven to 475F.

2. Peel garlic. Place cloves on aluminum foil square. Drizzle with 1 tbsp. oil. Sprinkle on several black pepper grindings. Enclose in foil. Pop packet in oven till the garlic becomes tender. This typically takes 20 minutes to 1/2 hour.

3. As garlic is roasting, trim, then chop mushrooms. You can slice them if you prefer.

4. Heat 2 tbsp. +/- of remaining oil in large sized fry pan on med-high. When oil has heated, add mushrooms and salt. Stir frequently while cooking till mushrooms release their own liquid, that liquid has cooked off and mushrooms begin browning. Remove from the heat. Set them aside.

5. Grate cheese. Chop mint.

6. When oven is hot, stretch dough to your thin-ness preference. Work with a half of the dough at one time. Place on oiled cookie sheet. Use 1/2 of the rest of the ingredients on each pizza.

7. Sprinkle with fontina cheese. Scatter mushrooms on top. Arrange garlic cloves around pizza evenly. Sprinkle with mint and parmesan cheese.

8. Brush on a little more oil. Grate some black pepper over whole pizza. Bake till crust has browned and cheese has melted. Repeat with the rest of your ingredients. Remove from oven and serve.

Conclusion

This mushroom-centric cookbook has shown you…

How to use different ingredients to enhance the taste of delicious mushrooms, in dishes both well-known and rare.

How can you include mushrooms in your home recipes?

You can…

- Make breakfast scrambles or omelets sprinkled liberally with mushrooms. They make excellent additions to breakfast dishes.
- Learn to cook with different types of mushrooms, widely used in in many areas of the world. Find special or rare mushrooms at European, Asian or home-grown type food markets if you don't see them at your local grocers or farmer's markets.
- Enjoy making the delectable mushroom and pasta dishes from many lands, like risotto and spaghetti. There are SO many ways to use mushrooms.
- Make soups using mushrooms. They play so well with the other ingredients that make tasty soups.

Have fun experimenting! Enjoy the results!

Printed in Great Britain
by Amazon